The MAILBOX®

The Education Center®

Colors

Preschool

W9-AHS-090

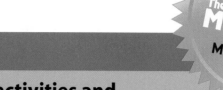

THE BEST OF The MAILBOX® MAGAZINE

Our best color activities and reproducibles from the 1998–2007 issues of *The Mailbox*® and *Teacher's Helper*® magazines

- **Literacy activities**
- **Learning centers**
- **Group-time activities**
- **Songs, poems, and fingerplays**

- **Math activities**
- **Arts-and-crafts ideas**
- **...and more!**

Fun and practical skills practice!

Managing Editor: Tina Petersen

Editorial Team: Becky S. Andrews, Diane Badden, Kimberley Bruck, Karen A. Brudnak, Pam Crane, Tazmen Hansen, Marsha Heim, Lori Z. Henry, Debra Liverman, Kitty Lowrance, Jennifer Nunn, Mark Rainey, Hope Rodgers, Rebecca Saunders, Rachael Traylor, Sharon M. Tresino, Zane Williard

www.themailbox.com

©2010 The Mailbox® Books
All rights reserved.
ISBN10 #1-56234-916-3 • ISBN13 #978-1-56234-916-5

Printed in the United States
10 9 8 7 6 5 4 3 2 1

HPS 212074

Table of Contents

Thematic Units

Build a variety of developmentally appropriate skills with these colorful activities, center ideas, songs, arts-and-crafts ideas, and classroom displays.

Reinforce basic skills with fun, ready-to-use practice pages.

A PALETTE OF COLORFUL LEARNING

Mix these ideas into your teaching and help paint a pretty picture about colors for your little ones.

ideas by Angie Kutzer, Garrett Elementary, Mebane, NC

COLORFUL LEIS
Identifying matching colors

There's a lot of lei switching going on during this color-matching game! Purchase a solid-colored plastic lei for each child so that half the class will have one color and the other half of the class will have another color. Instruct each child to wear her lei as you play some lively music. Stop the music at random and have each youngster switch leis with someone whose lei is the same color. Periodically during play, review the colors of the leis. As more colors are introduced, add new sets of leis to the game. Hey, we're both wearing yellow!

I'm learning my colors.
Yes, it's true.

This bouquet has more colors
Than one or two.

Let me name each one
For you!

A BLOOMING BOUQUET OF COLOR
Identifying colors

These bouquets will make lovely refrigerator works of art and will also help little ones learn their colors! To prepare, make a copy of the vase pattern on page 6 for each child. Gather several different colors of artificial flowers, and provide a shallow dish of corresponding paint for each bloom.

Have each youngster color his vase pattern. Help each child cut out the vase pattern and glue it to the bottom of a 12" x 18" sheet of construction paper. Have him use a green crayon to draw stems and leaves coming out of the vase. Next, instruct him to choose a flower and dip it in the matching paint color. Have him make prints on his paper, as shown, in three or more different colors. Encourage him to use three or four different blooms for a vivid display. After each child finishes, have him tell you which colors he used in his painting. Beautiful!

COLORFUL BUILDINGS

Identifying colors

This activity integrates listening skills, positional concepts, *and* color identification! In advance, gather 15 blocks—five each of three different colors. Give each child in a small group of four a set of three differently colored blocks. Use the remaining set to demonstrate how to build a tower. After some free exploration, hold up a sheet of paper or a book so that the students can't see your tower. Create a tower with two of the blocks and describe it to the children. For example, you might say, "My tower is red and yellow." Then instruct students to build towers like the one you described. Reveal your tower to students and have each youngster check to see if she made a match. As play continues, increase the level of difficulty by using all three blocks and naming specific positions for each one: top, middle, and bottom. We're breaking ground on new skills!

SUPER LOOPS

Sorting colors

Here's an alternative to using beads and laces at your fine-motor center that adds some practice with sorting by color. Empty a box of Froot Loops cereal into a container. Place pipe cleaners that correspond to the cereal's colors in the emptied box. To complete this activity, a child picks two or three pipe cleaners and threads the correct color of cereal onto each one. After he shows his work to an adult, have him remove the cereal from the pipe cleaners and return it to the bowl to ready the center for the next visitor. Be sure to have some fresh cereal on hand for students to snack on when this super center is finished.

BUBBLE GUM, BUBBLE GUM
Naming colors, identifying colors

This adaptation of a traditional jump rope chant gets your youngsters calling out color names! To prepare, put a supply of large pom-poms into a clear fishbowl. Chant the rhyme shown; then call out a student's name at the end. Have him name a color of gumball he'd like to have, and then invite him to take a pom-pom from the bowl. Continue in this manner until everyone has had a turn.

Bubble gum, bubble gum in a dish.

For which color of gumball do you wish?

OVER THE RAINBOW
Naming colors

Youngsters learn all the colors to reach this pot of gold! Gather a sheet of construction paper in each of the following basic colors: red, orange, yellow, green, blue, purple, black, and brown. Tape them to the floor in order, creating a rainbowlike path. At the end of the path, place a plastic cauldron (found in discount stores during Halloween) filled with gold-wrapped chocolate coin candy. When a child is ready to recite all of the colors, have her start at the beginning of the path and name each color as she steps on it. If she makes it to the end of the path, naming all of the colors correctly, reward her with a piece of gold!

A COLOR-MIXING PALETTE
Mixing colors

Get ready for lots of oohs and aahs when you show your youngsters this color display! To prepare, make three transparency copies of page 7. Use permanent markers to color each copy as shown. Place the blue copy on your overhead projector. Point to the color word and read it aloud. Next, place the red copy over the blue and read the corresponding color words. Finally, add the yellow copy and finish reading. Follow up this activity by letting budding artists paint and do some color mixing of their own!

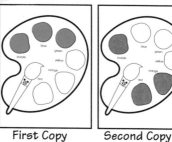

First Copy (Color blue.)	**Second Copy** (Color red.)	**Third Copy** (Color yellow.)

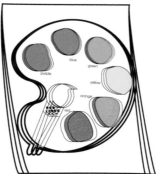

Vase Pattern
Use with "A Blooming Bouquet of Color" on page 3.

I'm learning my colors.
Yes, it's true.

This bouquet has more colors
Than one or two.

Let me name each one
For you!

TEC61248

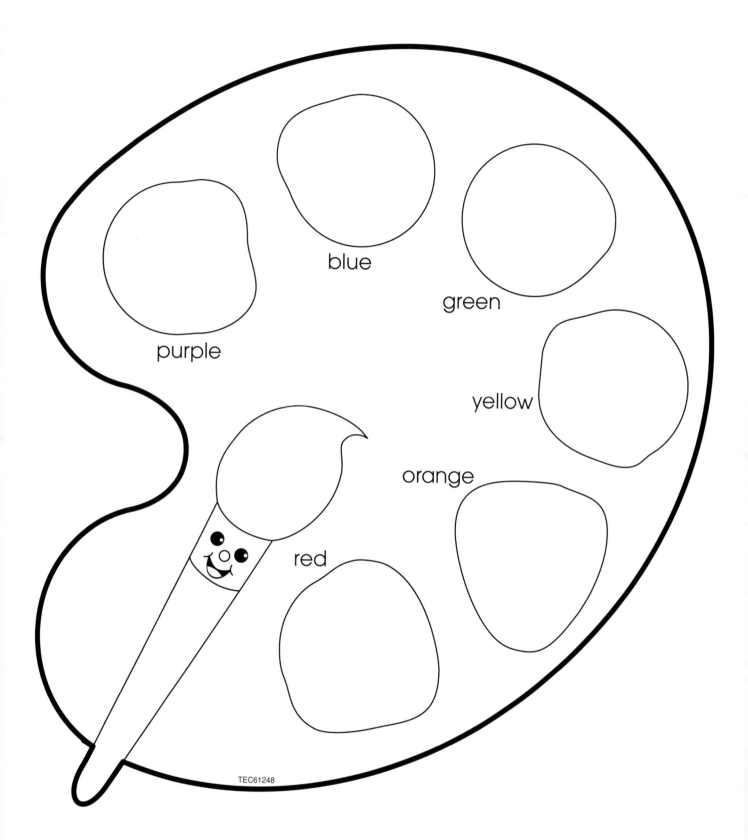

purple

blue

green

yellow

orange

red

TEC61248

A Closetful of Colorful Monster Ideas

Use these friendly monster ideas to help teach your preschoolers all about colors. Your little ones will be experts before you can say "Boo!"

Group Time

There Are Monsters in Here!

Youngsters will be tickled pink when you begin your color study with this amusing monster hunt. In advance, photocopy the patterns on page 13 to create nine monsters. Color the monsters the same color. Laminate them and then cut out each one. Before students arrive in the morning, hide the monsters around your classroom. Then begin your group time by singing the first verse of the song shown. Invite students to find the hidden monsters and then bring them back to the circle. Display the monsters. Count them with your youngsters and then sing the second verse of the song. For an added challenge, hide several sets of monsters in different colors. Sing the song and have students find only the colored monsters mentioned in the song.

(sung to the tune of "Ten Little Indians")

One [red], two [red], three [red] monsters.
Four [red], five [red], six [red] monsters.
Seven [red], eight [red], nine [red] monsters.
Find where they're hiding right now!

One [red], two [red], three [red] monsters.
Four [red], five [red], six [red] monsters.
Seven [red], eight [red], nine [red] monsters.
We found where they were hiding!

Cele McCloskey, Head Start of York County, York, PA

Movement

Monster Movements

To prepare for this musical monster activity, cut out large construction paper monster feet in a variety of colors. Be sure each foot is large enough for one or two children to stand on. Laminate the feet and then tape each one to the floor of your circle-time area. Play a lively musical selection, such as "The Monster Mash," and invite students to dance to the music. Stop the music. Call out a color and direct each child to stand on a footprint in that color. Those monsters sure do have big feet!

Angie Kutzer
Burlington, NC

Five Little Monsters

Thrill your youngsters with this monster mitt and poem! To make a mitt, gather five pom-poms in five different colors. Glue a pair of wiggle eyes to each pom-pom and then use self-adhesive Velcro fasteners to attach them to an old glove as shown. During your group time, slip on the monster mitt and begin reciting the poem below. Five little monsters…

Five little monsters sitting on the floor.
The [red] one said, "Let's knock on someone's door."
The [green] one said, "Let's act a little scary."
The [white] one said, "Why are we so hairy?"
The [blue] one said, "I hear a funny sound."
The [pink] one said, "There's no one else around."
Then "WOOSH" went the wind and "EEK!" someone said.
So five little monsters ran under the bed.

craft idea by
Lori Burrow, Meridian, CA

Purple Hair, Yellow Eyes…

If you could make a monster, what would it look like? Use this small-group activity as a stand-alone idea or as a follow-up to Ed Emberley's book *Go Away, Big Green Monster!* To prepare, use different-colored permanent markers to draw a monster face outline and monster features, each on a separate overhead transparency (as shown). Set up an overhead projector and place the monster face transparency on it. Invite each child in the group to choose a feature and place it on the projector. When the face is complete, review the different-colored features on the monster. Then remove the features from the projector one by one. Bye-bye purple hair!

Angie Kutzer
Burlington, NC

Fingerpainting, Monster Style

It's true! Monsters love fingerpainting just as much as preschoolers do! So invite your youngsters to try this color-mixing activity—the monster way. To make one monster masterpiece, invite a child to wear a set of plastic monster fingertips or fingernails (available at party supply stores). Provide the child with a sheet of fingerpaint paper and two spoonfuls of fingerpaint that will blend to make another color. Drop the paint onto the paper and direct the child to use her monster fingers to mix the colors together. What fiendish fun!

adapted from an idea by
Lori Burrow
Meridian, CA

This Monster Says...

Identifying colors will be a scream with this lively song and activity! In advance, duplicate the monster patterns on page 13 to create a class supply. Have each child color a monster one color and then tape a craft stick to the back of it. During circle time, invite a child to show his monster stick puppet to the group. Have the class identify the color; then encourage your youngsters to join the monster in singing the song shown. (For the colors purple, yellow, and orange, sing the variation.) After singing the last line, invite the child to tell the class what his monster says. Continue the activity until each child has had a chance to show off his monster. Boo!

(sung to the tune of "Alouette")

I'm a monster.
I'm a big [blue] monster.
I'm a monster.
And this is what I say…

Variation:
I'm a monster.
I'm a [purple] monster.
I'm a monster.
And this is what I say…

The Better to See You With!

What's the best part of a great big monster? His great big eyes! Create a set of monster-eye manipulatives by painting different-colored irises on Ping-Pong balls. When the paint is dry, invite students to sort the eyes by color into clean, empty egg cartons. The eyes have it!

Lori Burrow
Meridian, CA

Furry Findings

Dogs and cats aren't the only ones that shed. Monsters do, too! Invite your youngsters to clean up after these critters with this color-matching idea. To prepare, duplicate the monster patterns on page 13. Color each monster a different color. Cut out the monsters and then glue each one onto a small paper bag. Place the bags near your sensory table; then fill the table with rice and lengths of yarn in the same colors as the monsters. Direct each child to sift through the rice to find lengths of "monster fur." Then have him place the fur in the matching monster bag. These monsters aren't scary—they're hairy!

Roxanne Dearman
North Carolina School for the Deaf
Charlotte, NC

Monster Cutups

This small-group activity reinforces color recognition, body-part recognition, and following directions. In advance, make different-colored copies of the monster pattern on page 14. Laminate the monsters and then cut apart each one on the bold lines. Set the patterns at a center and invite three children to the area. To begin the activity, direct each child to find a different-colored monster part. For example, ask one child to find blue feet, one child to find a yellow body, and one child to find a green head. Then have the group work together to assemble the colorful creature. When students are familiar with this activity, invite a pair of children to use the center independently. Have one child give directions to the other child; then have them switch roles. "Make a monster with purple feet, a green body, and an orange head!"

Ada Goren
Winston-Salem, NC

11

Monsters Lay Eggs, Too!

Color-matching skills will be hatching at this fine-motor center. To prepare, gather several plastic Easter eggs in a variety of colors. Next, make a matching monster for each egg by gluing paper eyes and felt features to a large pom-pom. Set the monsters and eggs at a center; then invite your youngsters to place each monster inside the matching egg.

adapted from an idea by
Roxanne Dearman
Charlotte, NC

Color Tracking

Keep track of which colors your youngsters have mastered with this assessment idea. To begin, duplicate the award on page 15 for each child. Program each award with a different child's name; then place the awards in an easily accessible location. Each time a child learns a new color, invite him to color the appropriate monster on his award. When the child has mastered all of the colors, encourage him to take the award home to show his family what he knows. Daddy and "Mummy" will be so proud!

"I Scream" Sundaes

Learning all those colors is a monstrous task! So wrap up your color unit by treating each child to a monster's favorite snack—an "I Scream" Sundae! To make one, place a scoop of lime sherbet in a plastic bowl. Add a squirt of whipped cream. Then top the sundae with some colored sprinkles and a Gummy worm. Have each child identify the colors in her sundae and then invite her to dig in. There's nothing scary about this snack, but it *will* give your youngsters the chills!

Lori Burrow
Meridian, CA

Monster Patterns

Use with "There Are Monsters in Here!" on page 8,
"This Monster Says…" on page 10, and "Furry Findings" on page 11.

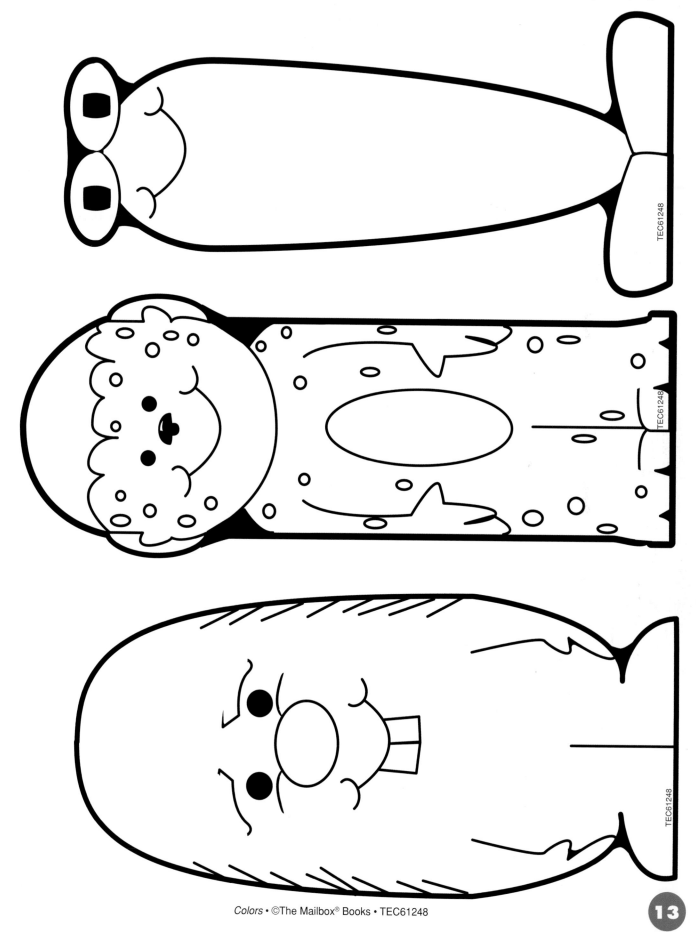

TEC61248

TEC61248

TEC61248

Monster Pattern
Use with "Monster Cutups" on page 11.

TEC61248

purple

orange

brown

black

Hooray!

_____

knows all of these colors!

white

blue

yellow

red

green

pink

Colors • ©The Mailbox® Books • TEC61248

Note to the teacher: Use with "Color Tracking" on page 12.

15

A Rainbow

Brighten up your classroom with this colorful collection of center ideas that are sure to please!

ideas contributed by Ada Goren, Winston-Salem, NC

Color Search
Matching colors

Each youngster contributes to this vivid tabletop rainbow! Tape colorful strips of bulletin board paper to a tabletop to resemble a rainbow. Place scissors, glue, and a supply of magazine pages (or grocery store circulars) at the table. A youngster looks through the pages to find pictures that match the colors of the strips. When she finds a picture, she cuts it out, identifies the color, and then glues it in place. Beautiful!

Rainbow Rubbings
Identifying letters

Write the word *rainbow* in black marker on several tagboard strips. Then trace the letters with thick lines of white glue. When the glue is dry, tape the strips to a tabletop. Stock the center with unwrapped crayons, tape, and a supply of white copy paper. A visiting child feels the letters and names any he recognizes. Then he tapes a sheet of paper on top of the strip (provide help with taping as needed). Finally, he rubs a variety of colorful crayons over the paper.

# of Centers

Writing Center

Color Favorites
Connecting spoken language with written words

Make a class supply of the poem pattern on page 19. Place the poems at a center along with 12" x 18" sheets of construction paper, crayons, and glue. Arrange for an adult to assist youngsters at this center. When a child visits the center, the adult reads the poem aloud and writes the youngster's dictated responses on the lines. Then the student glues her poem to the bottom half of a sheet of construction paper and draws corresponding pictures above the poem as shown.

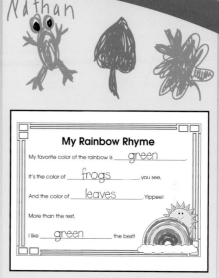

Nathan

My Rainbow Rhyme

My favorite color of the rainbow is _green_.

It's the color of _frogs_, you see,

And the color of _leaves_. Yippee!

More than the rest,

I like _green_ the best!

Snack Center

Cup of Colors
Following directions

This fruity snack serves up a rainbow of colors! Place at a center separate bowls of strawberry slices, mandarin orange sections, pineapple pieces, green grape halves, blueberries, and purple-tinted whipped topping. A child places a tablespoon of each fruit in a clear plastic cup and then tops it with a scoop of whipped topping. What a tasty rainbow!

Sensory Center

Scoop and Search
Using the sense of touch to explore objects

Fluffy clouds are hidden in this rainbow of rice! To prepare, mix a small amount of rubbing alcohol and food coloring in a large resealable plastic bag. Then add rice and shake the bag until it is thoroughly coated. Pour the rice on paper towels to dry. Prepare several additional colorful batches of rice in the same manner. Pour the prepared rice in a large plastic tub and mix in several cotton ball clouds. Place near the tub several sieves with large holes. A child chooses a sieve and then uses it to scoop up some of the mixture. As the rice funnels through the sieve, it leaves behind the fluffy clouds!

adapted from an idea by Teresa Gmerek, Glendale Head Start, Flinton, PA

Colorful Collage Headband
Using a variety of media

Youngsters showcase their favorite colors with this vibrant headband. Place at a center a supply of colorful construction paper strips labeled with color words as shown. Also provide access to glue and a variety of craft materials, such as tissue paper, sticky dots, gift ribbon, and craft feathers. A child chooses a strip and then glues materials of the same color to the strip. When the glue is dry, size the strip to fit the child's head. These creative headbands are the tops!

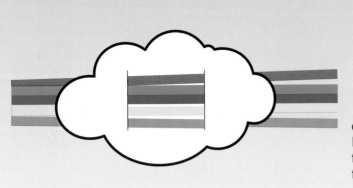

Cloud Weaving
Developing fine-motor skills

This simple weaving project is a visual delight! For each child, make two parallel cuts in a large cloud cutout as shown. Place the clouds and a large supply of colorful construction paper strips at a center. A child weaves as many strips through the cloud as desired. Then he glues the strips in place (provide assistance with gluing as needed).

Toss the Rainbow
Developing gross-motor skills

To make a rainbow tossing toy, poke a hole through the lid of a film canister. Thread colorful lengths of curling ribbon through the hole. Then knot the ribbons together under the lid and snap it on the canister. Attach two large cloud cutouts to your floor, making sure they are several feet apart. Place the canister on a cloud. A pair of students visits the center, and each child stands behind a different cloud. One child tosses the rainbow toward his partner's cloud. The other youngster retrieves the rainbow and tosses it back toward the other cloud. Students continue tossing the rainbow as time allows.

My Rainbow Rhyme

My favorite color of the rainbow is _____.

It's the color of _____, you see,

And the color of _____. Yippee!

More than the rest,

I like _____ the best!

Note to the teacher: Use with "Color Favorites" on page 17.

My Many Colored Days

Written by Dr. Seuss

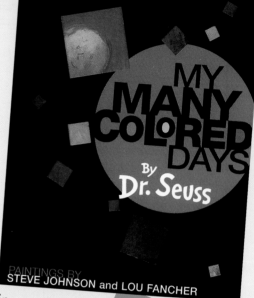

PAINTINGS BY
STEVE JOHNSON and LOU FANCHER

Your youngsters will be filled with feeling when you share this book about colorful kinds of emotions. After reading the story, use the following story extensions to help students further explore their emotions.

ideas contributed by Lucia Kemp Henry

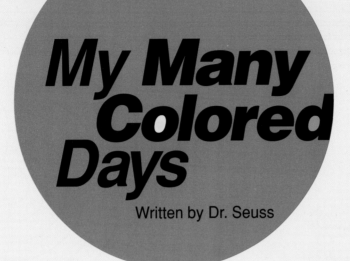

My Many Colored Feelings

After the initial reading of this lively book, your youngsters will jump at the chance to act out the emotions depicted in the story. To begin, have a small group of students stand in front of the class. Begin reading the book, and invite the group to demonstrate each emotion as described in the story. As you read about a "Mixed-Up Day," encourage students to create their own actions describing the feeling. Repeat the activity throughout the week until each child has had a chance to dramatize the book. If desired, have your entire class practice acting out the story and then perform the drama for another class. *Literature experience, emotional awareness*

A Multicolored Day

A single day brings different feelings to different people. Help your preschoolers explore this concept with a colorful graphing activity. In advance, prepare a graph similar to the one shown. During your group time, say the following chant. Have each child place her photograph in the column that describes her mood; then discuss the graph with your youngsters. Repeat the activity daily for one week and your preschoolers will soon see how one day can be many colors. *Graphing, emotional awareness*

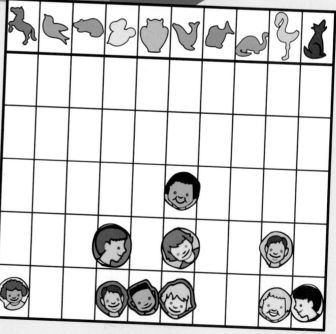

On this many colored day,
We all might feel a different way!
Yellow, orange, purple, gray.
What color do you feel today?

Keeping a Colorful Journal

Now that your youngsters have focused on feelings in a group, it's time for each child to record his mood in a personalized journal! In advance, make five copies of the journal pattern on page 22. Program each pattern with a different day from Monday through Friday. (Or adjust the days on the journal pages as needed.) Photocopy the programmed pages to make a set for each child. Staple the pages in sequence between construction paper covers; then add a title to each child's journal similar to the one shown.

To begin the activity, have each child review his color on the group graph. (See "A Multicolored Day" on page 20.) Then have him find the day's page in his journal and color the character to match the graph. Invite the child to dictate a sentence or two about his feelings; then write his response on his journal page. At the end of the week, have your preschoolers read their journals and review their different moods. Wow! We really do have many colored days!

Literacy, expressing feelings

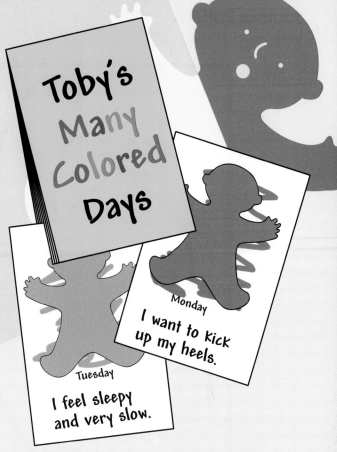

Toby's Many Colored Days

Monday
I want to kick up my heels.

Tuesday
I feel sleepy and very slow.

Picture a Feeling

Encourage your preschoolers to explore feelings a little further with an activity that helps them read the emotions of others. To prepare, cut out magazine pictures that show people expressing the different moods mentioned in the book. Then glue each picture onto a colored piece of paper. Show each picture, in turn, to a small group of students. Invite youngsters to discuss what the person in the picture might be feeling and why she might feel that way.

Recognizing the feelings of others, language development

Acting It Out

How will your youngsters feel about these colorful stick puppets? They'll be tickled pink! Use the figure from the journal pattern on page 22 and the animal patterns on pages 22 and 23 to make tagboard tracers. Then use the tracers to make tagboard cutouts similar to the ones shown. Tape a craft stick to the back of each cutout. Place the puppets at your puppet theater, and invite each child to use the props to create a many colored show about feelings. ***Dramatic play, language development***

Journal Pattern
Use with "Keeping a Colorful Journal" and "Acting It Out" on page 21.

Animal Patterns
Use with "Acting It Out" on page 21.

TEC61248

TEC61248

TEC61248

TEC61248

TEC61248

TEC61248

TEC61248

TEC61248

TEC61248

Mouse Paint

Written and Illustrated by Ellen Stoll Walsh

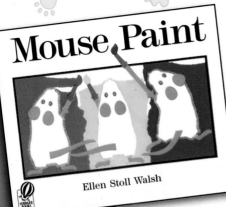

Mouse Paint
Ellen Stoll Walsh

Three white mice standing on a white piece of paper are nearly invisible to a lurking cat. But when the mice discover jars of red, yellow, and blue paint, they partake in some risky color mixing! No doubt these color-conscious rodents will remember that the cat is still hovering nearby.

ideas contributed by Roxanne LaBell Dearman
Western NC Early Intervention Program for Children Who Are Deaf or Hard of Hearing
Charlotte, NC

Almost Invisible!
Building prior knowledge

Introduce youngsters to the concept of camouflage with this engaging prereading activity! Cut out a copy of the mouse pattern on page 26, making sure to completely trim off the bold outer line. Tape the mouse to a sheet of white construction paper and then display the paper near your large-group area. To begin, express dismay at how difficult it is to see the white mouse on white paper. Encourage youngsters to suggest ways they could make the mouse show up more, such as coloring him red or placing him on a blue sheet of paper. Then explain that your storytime selection for the day is about three white mice that hide from a cat on a sheet of white paper.

Dance, Dance, Dance!
Expressing oneself through art

The brightly colored mice are shocked when their dancing feet mix up puddles of secondary colors. No doubt your little ones will want to try some mixing fun as well! For each child, place dollops of red, yellow, and blue paint on a 12" x 18" sheet of white construction paper. Then give each youngster three cotton balls to resemble mice. Play a recording of upbeat music and have little ones dance their mice through the paint. That little mouse made the color green!

Mixing Colors
Developing color recognition

Little ones brush up on color recognition with this nifty rhyme. Use the pattern on page 26 to make a mouse cutout in each of the following colors: blue, yellow, and red. Make a matching puddle cutout for each mouse. Next, attach the red mouse and blue puddle to your board as shown. Lead students in reciting the rhyme below. Then invite them to guess the color that results from mixing red and blue paint, reviewing the book's illustrations if needed. Continue in the same way with other combinations of mice and puddles, replacing the color word in the first line of the rhyme each time.

Dance little [red] mouse; stomp your feet.
Wiggle your tail as you feel the beat.
Then look down; don't be afraid
To find out what new color you've made!

The blue mouse is hiding on the blue bookcase.

Hide-and-Seek
Developing connections between spoken and written words

Where should a little mouse hide from a hungry cat? Why, on something the same color as its fur, of course! Have each child color and cut out a copy of the mouse pattern on page 26. Next, help each youngster think of a good hiding place for the mouse. For example, a blue mouse could hide very nicely on a blue bookcase. Have the child observe as you write a sentence on a matching strip of paper to explain where the mouse is hiding. Then help the child attach the mouse to the location indicated. Look at all the mice hiding in the classroom!

25

Preschool Painters

Listening for the beginning sound /p/

No painting smocks are needed for this unique whole-group activity! Give each child a clean paintbrush and a copy of page 27. Encourage students to say the word *paint* several times, leading them to notice that the word begins with the /p/ sound. Then have students locate the picture of the pig and say its name, emphasizing the /p/ sound. Guide students to conclude that the word *paint* and the word *pig* both begin with the /p/ sound. Then encourage students to brush their paintbrushes over the pig while repeating the /p/ sound a few times. Repeat the process with each picture on the page. If desired, encourage each youngster to take his paper home to color with his family.

Name MiKayla

Painting Pictures

Listen for directions.

Beginning sound /p/

Mouse Pattern

Use with "Almost Invisible!" on page 24 and "Mixing Colors" and "Hide-and-Seek" on page 25.

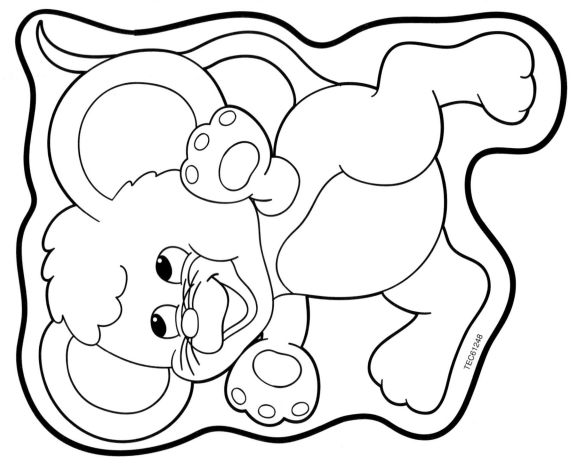

TEC61248

Painting Pictures

Listen for directions.

Note to the teacher: Use with "Preschool Painters" on page 26.

ART EXPLORATION

An introduction to the language of art and its basic elements gives young children a voice for self-expression and a source for creative exploration. Art experiences improve visual discrimination skills, strengthen prereading and premath skills, increase verbal abilities, encourage creativity, and give children opportunities to develop a lifelong love of art.

ideas contributed by Lori Kent

EXPLORING THE ELEMENT OF COLOR

ALL ABOUT COLOR

You know that you need to teach youngsters colors. But do you know what you can teach them *about* colors?

- Brighten up their vocabularies by using these terms in your everyday exploration of color: *Hue* is the name of a color; *value* refers to how light or dark a color is.
- Color mixing is like magic. If you add black to a color, you change its *shade*. If you add white, you change its *tint*. Combinations of two of the colors red, blue, or yellow result in new colors: orange, green, and violet.
- Colors have families. We call yellow, orange, and red the warm family. Green, blue, and violet make up the cool family.

COLOR COPTERS

Color mixing and patterning skills take flight when your little ones propel these cool color copters into the air. To make one, cut a circle from tagboard that is 3½" in diameter. Use a black marker to visually divide the circle into eight sections as shown. Have a child alternately color the sections two primary colors. Next, cut three slits in one end of a straw to create tabs. Use tape to secure the tabs to the uncolored side of the circle. To make his copter take flight, a child holds the straw between the palms of his hands and quickly rubs his palms in opposite directions. He then lets go of the straw by separating his hands. Encourage the child to observe the colors blending together as the color copter spins and then takes flight.

COLORFUL LANGUAGE

light	color wheel
dark	color families
value	shade
bright	tint
mix	warm
blend	cool
hue	neutral

SHOW YOUR COLORS

Improve youngsters' visual discrimination skills, color-recognition skills, *and* sorting abilities with this center activity. Obtain different colors of paint samples from a home-supplies or paint store. Cut the samples apart; then put them in a center. Encourage a child to find all of the pieces of the same color. Then help her arrange the pieces from lightest to darkest.

AROUND THE COLOR WHEEL

Introduce your little ones to the color wheel with this movement activity. To make a giant color wheel, cut a large circle from each of the following colors of laminated construction paper: red, orange, yellow, green, blue, and violet. Arrange the colors in a circle on the floor of your group area; then secure them with double-sided tape. To play, ask each of six children to stand on a different color. Sing the following song as the group moves in one direction around the circle. At the end of the first verse, have the children stop and stand on the circles. Each time you sing the second verse, name two colors. Direct the children standing on those colors to dance together inside the circle. Here we go!

Here We Go Round the Color Wheel
(sung to the tune of "The Mulberry Bush")

Here we go round the color wheel, the color wheel, the color wheel.
Here we go round the color wheel; the colors make a circle.

[Red] and [green] please step inside, step inside, step inside.
[Red] and [green] please step inside; dance inside the circle.

SQUISHY COLOR COMBOS

Get your little ones set for some squishing and squashing fun as they explore color mixing with this small-group project. Obtain two or more identically sized pieces of clear vinyl or plastic table covering (available from fabric stores). Put one piece on a tile floor or on a tabletop. Randomly drop blobs of two different colors of either red, yellow, or blue paint onto the vinyl piece. Place the second piece atop the first. Encourage several children to use their fingers to rub the top piece of vinyl to mix the colors together to create a new color. To reuse the vinyl pieces, simply rinse them off. Introduce youngsters to tints by placing white paint and any other color of paint between the vinyl layers. Create new shades of colors by having youngsters mix together black and one color between the layers.

A COLOR DIP

Your little ones will be anxious to dip into this center to explore colors. Protect a tabletop with newspaper. Fill each section of a muffin tin with water; then use food coloring to tint the water different colors. Place the muffin tin and a roll of paper towels in the center. A youngster visiting the center puts on an apron. Next, she tears off a paper towel and folds it twice to make a square. She then repeatedly dips her paper towel into different colors of water until it is covered with color. If desired, display the dried towels together to create a quilt that evidences the colorful exploration.

BOOKS OF MANY COLORS

Color Dance
Written & Illustrated by Ann Jonas

Cat's Colors
Written & Illustrated by Jane Cabrera

Colors Everywhere
Photographed by Tana Hoban

Science

Mixing Up Colors

Little ones whip up secondary colors with this vivid investigation!

by Suzanne Moore, Tucson, AZ

Tint each of three containers of whipped topping a different primary color. Gather a small group of youngsters and present the whipped topping. Encourage students to identify the colors.

Place dollops of blue and yellow whipped topping in a bowl. Ask youngsters to predict what will happen when the two colors are mixed.

Repeat Steps 2 and 3 with yellow and red whipped topping and with blue and red whipped topping.

Give each child slices of fruit and dollops of green, purple, and orange whipped topping. Invite each child to dip her fruit into these tasty secondary colors and then nibble on her snack.

Explorations

To explore color mixing, you will need the following:
3 small containers of whipped topping
red, yellow, and blue food coloring (gel food coloring works best)
3 bowls
3 spoons
a small paper plate for each child
fruit slices for each child

STEP 3

Invite a child to stir the whipped topping as the remaining youngsters observe.

STEP 4

It's green!

When the colors are completely mixed, encourage children to identify the new secondary color.

Did You Know?

Some animals can't see certain colors. In fact, it's thought that dogs see the world in shades of just one color!

What Now?

Experiment with some chilly color mixing! Place water in the sections of an ice cube tray and then tint the water primary colors (yellow, blue, and red). Have each child choose two cubes in different colors and place them in a glass of clear soda. As the ice melts, the soda transforms into a secondary color!

Rainbow Ice
Water table

Is the ice melting outside? It'll be melting inside with this very colorful activity! To prepare, fill a bucket nearly full of water; then freeze it. Put the block of ice in your water table. Then prepare three containers of salted water: one red, one blue, and one yellow. Have your students use eyedroppers to drop the colored water onto the ice block. Have them observe how the salt water melts the ice, creating craters in the ice block. They'll also see how the colors of water blend to create new shades. Cool!

JoAnn Brukiewa
St. Clare School
Baltimore, MD

Our Favorite Colors
Graphing

Make the most of your youngest preschoolers' paintings with this paint-center idea. Near your easel prepare a display area titled "Our Favorite Colors." When a child paints a sheet of art paper one color, offer to cut the paper into a paintbrush shape when it is dry. Group the paintbrushes by color along with the painters' names.

adapted from an idea by Betsy Ruggiano
Featherbed Lane School
Clark, NJ

Ideas ● ● ● ● ● ● ● ●

Stained Glass Windows
Art

Looking for a craft to help youngsters learn about colors, color mixing, and shapes? Try this sticky version of stained glass! To make one stained glass window, use loops of tape to attach a square of clear Con-Tact paper to a tabletop (adhesive-side up). Provide a child with several shapes cut from red, yellow, and blue cellophane. Have her stick the shapes onto the Con-Tact paper to make a collage, overlapping the shapes as desired. Seal her finished collage by covering it with a sheet of clear Con-Tact paper. To create a frame for the window, staple strips of construction paper (in the child's choice of colors) to the four edges. Then hang these see-through creations in a sunny window. Wow!

Sherry Gish
Highland Plaza United Methodist Preschool and Kindergarten
Hixson, TN

Blend a Rainbow
Art

To make one of these unique rainbows, drop spoonfuls of red, orange, yellow, green, blue, and purple fingerpaint onto a large sheet of white paper. Be sure the drops of paint are in a line and close together. Cover the paint drops with a large sheet of waxed paper; then press and rub the paint so that the drops blend into one another. When the paint is dry, peel away the waxed paper and then cut out the rainbow. What a colorful sight!

Michele Menzel
Appleton, WI

Rainbow Crayons
Art

Youngsters will quickly learn the colors in a rainbow with this idea. Gather crayons in the following colors: red, orange, yellow, green, blue, and purple. Line up the crayons as shown; then tape them together with masking tape. Invite each child to use the line of crayons to draw an arch. Then have him identify the different colors. "Red, orange, yellow, green, blue, and purple. That must be a rainbow!"

Nancy Wolfgram
KinderCare Learning Center #IIII
Lincoln, NE

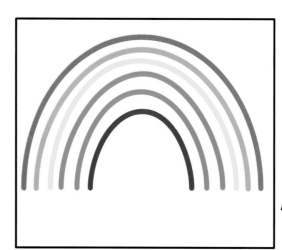
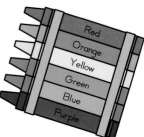

Color Wizardry
Science

Put a touch of color-mixing magic into your classroom with these manipulative bags. To prepare a bag, squirt a large dollop of shaving cream into a resealable plastic bag. Add drops of food coloring in two different primary colors to the bag. Close the bag, removing as much air as possible. Encourage a child to squeeze the bag until a new color appears. It's magic!

Joyce Anderson
Jewish Community Center of Greater Minneapolis
Minneapolis, MN

Swirling Rainbow
Science

This science recipe creates a magical mix of swirling colors! Cover the bottom of a pan with powdered milk. Carefully pour in room-temperature water until it is about $1/2$ inch from the top of the pan. Let the mixture stand until the water stops moving. Squeeze a few drops of several colors of food coloring into the milky mixture. Say some magic words; then add a few drops of liquid soap. Watch the colors swirl and twirl!

Vail McCole
Tiger's Treehouse
Grand Junction, CO

Color Palette
Circle time

Create an artist's palette and then send your youngsters off to paint the town—or actually, the classroom! To make the palette, cut an indented oval shape from white poster board. Use markers to color six circles, making each circle a different color you want students to recognize. At circle time, give each child a clean paintbrush. Point to one of the colors on your palette; then ask each child to find an item of the same color in your classroom. Once she finds an item, she pretends to paint it with her brush! After a few strokes, everyone should return to the circle for a new color-painting assignment!

Betsy Gaynor
Creative Nursery School
Naperville, IL

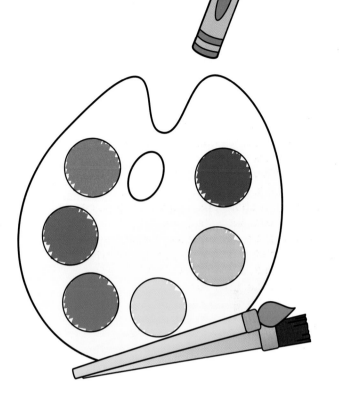

This is yellow.

Color Search
Circle time

Try this quick and easy game to reinforce color recognition! To begin, name a specific color and send preschoolers in search of classroom objects of this color. Tell each child to tap the object he finds, quietly name it, and return to the circle before you finish counting to 25. Then, one by one, invite students to show the class the objects they've identified. Playing this game at the beginning of the school year also familiarizes your little ones with their new classroom!

Amy Shimelman
Jewish Community Association of Austin
Early Childhood Program
Austin, TX

Color Toss!
Circle time

This simple beanbag toss is sure to be a hit. Gently toss a beanbag to a child, identifying the color of the beanbag and the child's name. For example, you might say, "I'm going to toss the [red] beanbag to my good friend [Bryan]." Then have him toss the beanbag back to you. Continue in this manner with other colors as you recognize each child in the group. What a fun way to acknowledge youngsters and help develop color recognition skills!

Lois Peterson
Mom's Day Out Christian Learning Center
Frederick, MD

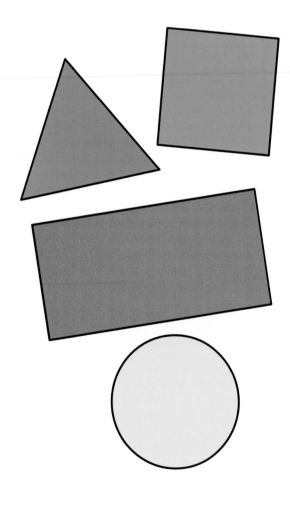

A Colorful Concoction
Circle time

Stir up some interest in colors with a pot of color soup! To prepare, cut out various simple shapes from different colors of construction paper. Label a box or basket with each color. Then hide the colorful shapes throughout your classroom. At circle time, ask youngsters to hunt for the shapes and sort them by color into the containers. To conclude the activity, dump all the shapes into a large pot and invite little ones to take turns stirring the pot of color soup with a big wooden spoon!

Once youngsters know their colors, relabel the containers to help your students concentrate on the shapes and make a pot of shape soup instead!

Pepper Leclerc
Merrimack Valley Christian Day School
Lowell, MA

Once Upon a Pea
Circle time

Searching for a pesky pea under a mound of mattresses will be so much fun that children are unlikely to notice they're working on color identification. From felt, cut a brown bed shape, a number of different-colored strips for the bed's mattresses, and one small pea. During circle time, introduce this activity by asking students to recall the story of *The Princess and the Pea*. Place the bed and mattresses on your flannelboard. Show the children the pea; then have them close their eyes while you hide it under a mattress. Invite youngsters to open their eyes and guess under which color mattress the pea is hidden. Remove mattresses as they are guessed until the pea is found. What royal guessers your preschoolers are!

Leslie Madalinski
Weekday Children's Center
Naperville, IL

Color Match
Circle time

This circle-time activity provides a basketful of color reinforcement. To make a color die for the activity, cover an empty square tissue box with white Con-Tact paper; then glue a different-colored circle to each side of the box. Next, fill a basket with a class supply of plastic eggs that are the same colors as those on the die. To begin the activity, give a child the basket of eggs. Invite her to roll the die and then find an egg that matches the color on the die. If a child rolls the die and there is not a matching egg, invite her to roll the die again. Continue playing the game until every child has an egg.

Rhonda Yates
Paso Robles, CA

Color Bowling
Circle time

This simple twist on soda-bottle bowling ties in basic skills of counting and color recognition. Into each of several clear, empty soda bottles, stuff a different color of tissue paper. Use whatever colors you wish to have students identify. Then set up the bottles and have youngsters bowl them over with a small ball. Once they've knocked down some bottles, have them count how many and tell you what colors they are.

Nancy Jandreau
Kids Corner Day Care
Potsdam, NY

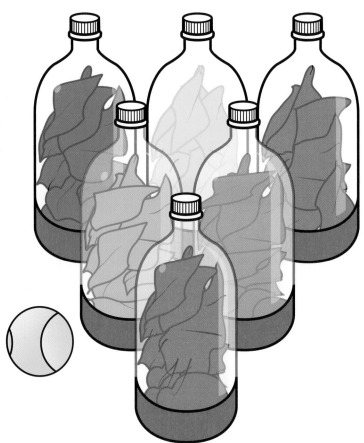

A Rainbow of Colors
Music

Transform a few sheets of construction paper into a bright rainbow when little ones act out this tune. First give each of six student volunteers a different color of construction paper—one red, one orange, one yellow, one green, one blue, and one purple. Arrange the children in front of your group from left to right in that order. Ask them to hold their papers in front of them and then turn around so that their backs are to the group. As each color is sung, tap the child holding it and have her turn around and hold her paper high. Look! It's a rainbow!

(sung to the tune of "Pop Goes the Weasel")

> Let's all name our colors right now.
> Red and orange and yellow.
> Green and blue and purple, too.
> Look! It's a rainbow!

Deborah Garmon, Groton, CT

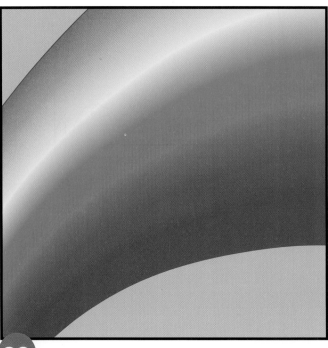

Brown Bear, Brown Bear, What Do You See?

This classic children's book by Bill Martin Jr. and Eric Carle is the perfect way to introduce your youngsters to various painting techniques while reinforcing color recognition. After reading the book, discuss the difference between an author and an illustrator; then examine Carle's illustrations. Next, focus on a different color each day as you have students use different techniques to paint outlines of animals that correspond to those in the book. For example, when you focus on yellow, have each child use a feather to paint a simple duck outline yellow. Or, when you focus on red, have each student paint liquid starch on a bird outline and then cover it with red tissue-paper squares. Other ideas include spatter-painting a frog outline green, sponge-painting a bear outline brown, fingerpainting a horse outline blue, or using small carpet squares to paint a cat outline purple. When a child has painted an animal to represent each one in the book, bind his pages together with a cover. If desired, add text similar to the book's to complete each child's own colorful book.

Betty Kabis Bissot
St. Anthony Cathedral School
Beaumont, TX

My Crayons Talk

Follow up a reading of *My Crayons Talk* by Patricia Hubbard with this crayon-box craft! To prepare, cut and fold a class supply of 12" x 18" yellow construction paper as shown. Decorate each folded paper to resemble a crayon box. Draw simple crayon shapes on a sheet of copy paper. Then duplicate the crayons onto eight basic shades of paper so that you have one crayon in each color per student. Cut out each set of eight crayons. (Older preschoolers can cut out the crayons themselves.)

Working with a small group, give each child one of the crayon boxes (unfolded) and one set of eight crayon shapes. Then say, "This color says, 'I am the color of a stop sign.' " Ask each youngster to find the crayon that is talking; then guide her to glue it on the far left side of the crayon box. Continue with other quotes from the crayons until she has glued all eight crayons in the box. Then demonstrate how to fold the box closed. Have youngsters take their crayon boxes home so they may share their color knowledge!

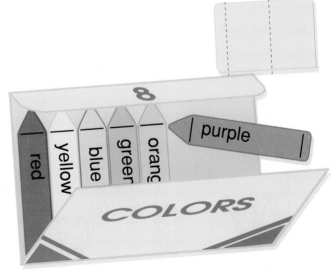

Anita Edlund
Cokesbury Children's Center
Knoxville, TN

Mary Wore Her Red Dress and Henry Wore His Green Sneakers

There are so many ways for children to enjoy this book by Merle Peek: singing the song, finding the new colors on each page, and retelling the story of Katy Bear's party! For even more fun, add story props—clothing that corresponds to the book. Either collect these items of children's clothing or cut them out of felt: red dress, green sneakers, yellow sweater, blue jeans, brown bandana, purple pants, violet ribbons, orange shirt, and pink hat. Then, as the group sings each verse of the story, have a child hang that piece of clothing on a clothesline. Sing the story again, this time asking children to remove the items as you sing the verses.

Katherine T. Brashears—Early Childhood Special Education
Enderly Heights Elementary
Buena Vista, VA

Color Dance

This color-exploration and art activity is the perfect follow-up to *Color Dance* by Ann Jonas. To prepare, cut out a supply of red, blue, and yellow cellophane shapes to represent scarves. Provide each child with a large sheet of white paper and three shapes, each in a different color. Direct the child to overlap the shapes and explore the colors created. When the child finds a combination of colors that he likes, invite him to glue the shapes onto the paper. If desired, have the child use crayons to draw dancers holding the shapes. What beautiful work! Take a bow!

Ellen Weiss
Fort Lauderdale, FL

Painting Pictures

Listen and do.

Note to the teacher: Use with the directions on page 44.

Painting Pictures

How to Use Page 43

Give each student a copy of page 43. Then read aloud the directions below to students.

Directions for Each Student

1. Color the boy's shirt purple.
2. Color the boy's pants blue.
3. Draw a brown dog on the paper attached to the easel.
4. Draw a yellow sun on the paper attached to the easel.
5. Draw an outlne of a cloud with your black crayon.

Finished Sample

Happy Spring!

Listen and do.

Note to the teacher: Use with the directions on page 46.

Happy Spring

How to Use Page 45

Give each student a copy of page 45. Then read aloud the directions below to students.

Directions for Each Student

1. Color the turtle shell brown and his body green.
2. Color the grass green.
3. Color the flower orange and the stem and leaves green.
4. Color the bee yellow.
5. Draw yourself in the grass wearing your favorite color.

Finished Sample

Colors and Shapes

Color by the code.

Color Code

△ — red

○ — yellow

□ — blue

▭ — green

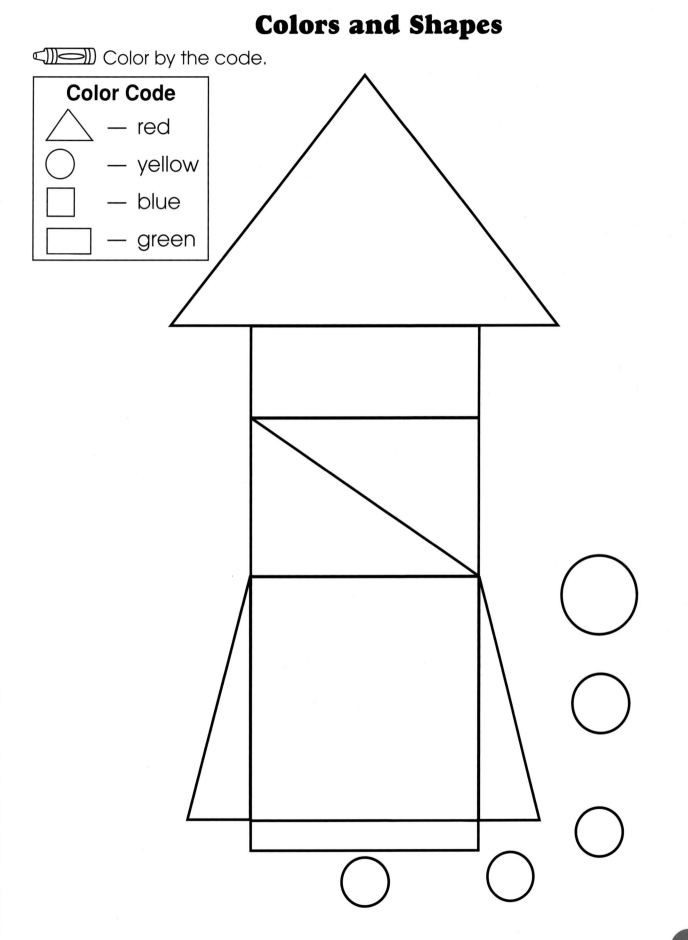

Just Beachy

Color the ⊕ green.

Color the ▱ blue.

Color the ☂ orange.

A B C D E F G H
I J K L M N O
26 P Q R S T U V
W X Y Z

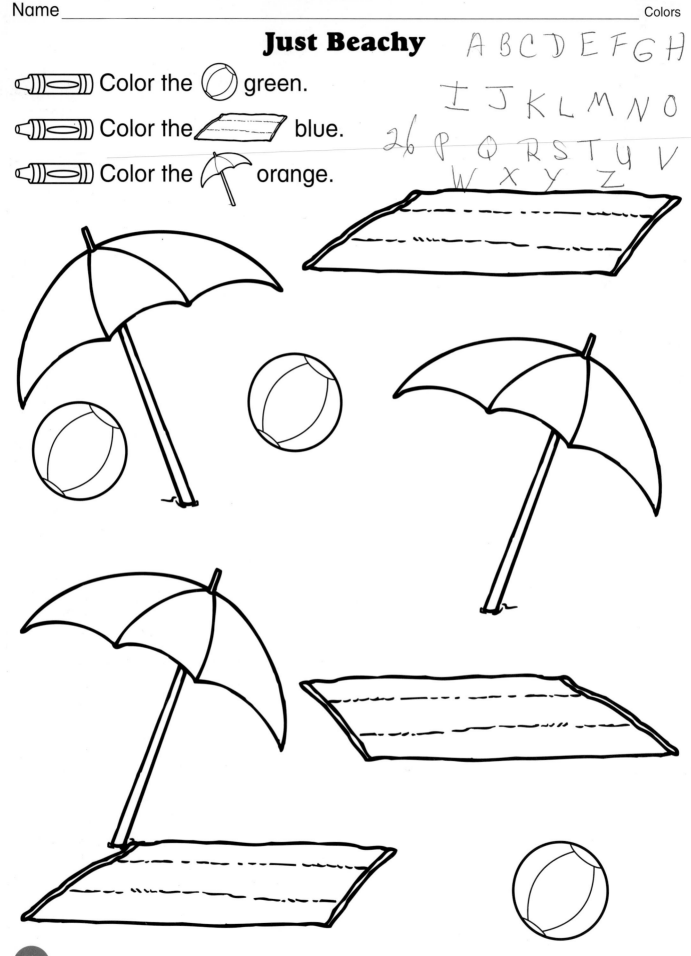